CHEF

COOL VOCATIONAL CAREERS

Published in the United States of America by Cherry Lake Publishing
Ann Arbor, Michigan
www.cherrylakepublishing.com

Content Adviser: Kristen Miglore, Creative Director at Food52 and author of *Food52 Genius Recipes: 100 Recipes That Will Change the Way You Cook*
Reading Adviser: Marla Conn MS, Ed., Literacy specialist, Read-Ability, Inc.

Photo Credits: © michaeljung/Shutterstock, cover, 1, 22; © Rich Legg/istock, 5; © bikeriderlondon/Shutterstock, 6; © Dmytro Zinkevych/istock, 8; © muratkoc/istock, 10; © cristianl/istock, 13; © Kzenon/Shutterstock, 14; © The Washington Post / Contributor / Getty Images, 16; © wavebreakmedia/Shutterstock, 18; © Roman Seliutin/Shutterstock, 21; © CandyBox Images, 24; © Helga Esteb/Shutterstock, 27; © Stockbyte/Thinkstock, 28

Library of Congress Cataloging-in-Publication Data
Names: Labrecque, Ellen, author.
Title: Chef / Ellen Labrecque.
Description: Ann Arbor : Cherry Lake Publishing, [2016] |
Series: Cool vocational careers | Audience: Grades 4 to 6.
Identifiers: LCCN 2015046656| ISBN 9781634710602 (hardcover) |
    ISBN 9781634712583 (pbk.) | ISBN 9781634711593 (pdf) | ISBN 9781634713573 (ebook)
Subjects: LCSH: Cooks—Juvenile literature. | Cooking—Vocational
    guidance—Juvenile literature.
Classification: LCC TX652.5 .L295 2016 | DDC 641.5023—dc23
LC record available at http://lccn.loc.gov/2015046656

Cherry Lake Publishing would like to acknowledge the work of the Partnership for 21st Century Learning.
Please visit *www.p21.org* for more information.

Printed in the United States of America
Corporate Graphics

ABOUT THE AUTHOR

Ellen Labrecque is a freelance writer living in Yardley, Pennsylvania. Previously, she was a senior editor at *Sports Illustrated Kids*. Ellen loves to travel and then learn about new places and people she can write about in her books.

TABLE OF CONTENTS

A Chef's Role

Arthur studied the **menu** in front of him. "I'm so hungry," he said. "I could eat everything on this menu."

"Well, you can't order *everything*," Arthur's mom said with a laugh. "But there are so many good choices here."

Arthur was out to dinner with his mom and dad. They were eating at their favorite Mexican restaurant. "I'll have the chicken tacos with guacamole," Arthur told the waiter. "Can I also have rice and beans on the side?"

"Of course," replied the waiter. He collected the menus after Arthur's parents ordered. "I'll be back soon with your dinner." He hurried to the kitchen with the order. The kitchen staff began to prepare a delicious meal for them.

A full meal at a restaurant might include many different foods.
Tacos are a popular Mexican food.

Chefs need to make sure the food looks appealing on the plate.

No matter what kind of restaurant you visit, there are people working hard in the kitchen to prepare tasty food. The restaurant business is a $683 billion industry! One out of every 10 American workers is in the restaurant business. The chef of the restaurant is in charge of most of these employees and works hard to make sure everything goes smoothly.

21st Century Content

Years ago, most of the chefs in top American restaurants were men. But this is no longer the case. More and more women are becoming chefs.

"A lot of jobs have tough schedules. A lot of jobs are physically demanding," said Lauren DeSteno, a chef in New York. "Nurses work weird hours. Police officers have hard jobs. You deal with it."

Today, up to 50 percent of the culinary staff is female. This is a much higher number than it was 10 years ago. More women are also graduating from the top culinary schools. At the Culinary Institute of America, female graduates rose from just 21 percent in 1992 to 36 percent today.

"In a good kitchen, male and female really doesn't matter anymore," DeSteno concluded.

Sushi is a popular Japanese food.

A chef is responsible for coming up with the recipes that are on the menu. Chefs use their taste and knowledge of food to decide which ingredients go best together. Many restaurants change their menus often. Some change their menus with the seasons. Other restaurants may have only a few choices on the menu at a time, so they change the menu every week. It is a chef's responsibility to make sure the menu makes sense. Chefs must think carefully about the style of food served at their restaurant. Picture a restaurant that specializes in **vegetarian** dishes. Would the owners be happy to find bacon on the menu? The appetizers and side dishes should **complement** the main courses. The meals should include a variety of tastes and **textures**. A very spicy side dish is not the best match for a very spicy main course. The chef also needs to decide how big each serving should be for every item on the menu. For chefs at fancier restaurants, creating the menu can be the biggest challenge of all. They use ingredients and cooking methods that many people might not be used to.

Chefs choose ingredients carefully. They want the food they prepare to be fresh and tasty. They must also make sure the ingredients are not too expensive. For example, a chef might want to use a rare spice in a new seafood dish. But the spice will make

Farms are a good source for fresh fruit and vegetables.

the dish very expensive. Will enough customers be willing to pay the high price? The chef may decide to use a less-expensive spice that will still work.

It is often the chef's job to purchase ingredients from suppliers. After planning the menu and deciding which ingredients will be needed, the chef places an order. Supply companies deliver the ingredients to the restaurant in big trucks. Meats, fruits and vegetables, and spices might all come from different companies.

Many **farm-to-table** chefs get some of their ingredients from the local farms in their area. Some restaurants even own the farm where the food is grown. No matter what type of restaurant it is, the chef always wants to get the best and freshest ingredients.

Chefs also need to keep their kitchens clean. They must follow any **health codes** that are set by local governments. Restaurants that do not follow these codes can be fined or shut down. Chefs must also make sure that food is cooked properly. People will not go back to restaurants that made them sick!

If chefs pay careful attention to all of this, they will likely be rewarded with many customers. Sometimes, chefs become so popular that people come from around the world to eat their food!

It Takes a Team

Chefs usually spend much of their time in kitchens. They must master a wide variety of cooking skills and methods. They trim meat to prepare it for cooking. They quickly chop vegetables and herbs. They must know how to create different kinds of sauces, doughs, and **marinades**. These can be just as important as meat and vegetables. What would a pizza be, for example, without a delicious crust?

Chefs use many tools to transform ingredients into meals. Knives come in different sizes, and there are many kinds of blades. Each type is designed for cutting certain foods. A short, stiff blade works well for removing bones from meat. A knife with a **serrated** edge can cut through soft foods, such as bread, without crushing them. Knowing which knife works best in each

A great pizza needs great ingredients.

A good chef knows how to use the stove safely.

situation is an important skill for any cook.

Knives aren't the only tools chefs use to cut ingredients. Grinders can turn meat into hamburger or sausage. Spice grinders can crush hard items such as peppercorns into powder for seasoning. Blenders and food processors can quickly cut ingredients very finely, so they can be used in soups and sauces.

It is also important for a chef to know which pots and pans are best for cooking different foods. A chef must choose the right type of cookware based on its shape and size. A chef must also understand the materials each piece of cookware is made of.

Aluminum and copper heat up quickly, but they do not hold heat well. This makes them good for cooking food that needs to get hot quickly, but not very good for slow cooking.

Knowing how to apply heat to food is often one of the most important and difficult cooking skills. After all, most people do not like to eat food that is burned or undercooked. Learning to tell when food is done cooking or needs to be turned over can take a lot of practice. Chefs learn how to cook using ovens, grills, stovetops, and other heating tools. Some recipes even call for the use of a small torch.

21st Century Content

Have you ever tried "Cherpumple"? Probably not! This crazy dessert was invented by the writer Charles Phoenix in 2009. It's a cherry pie, a pumpkin pie, and an apple pie all baked into a three-layer cake. He says that it's a good way to combine all of the desserts his family makes for Thanksgiving. "Since I always want to have a piece of each of the pies and the cake I figured why not make that waaaaaaaay more convenient," he wrote. "So I baked them all together as one and the Cherpumple was born."

Sous vide is an efficient way to cook meat.

Many chefs today use a popular process called **sous vide**. The food, usually meat, is sealed in a vacuum bag inside a water bath. This allows the meat to slowly cook without becoming overcooked or undercooked. "Technology like sous vide takes a lot of the guesswork out of the cooking process," explains one chef.

Most chefs specialize in a certain kind of **cuisine**. Sometimes, they stick to the traditions of a **regional** cuisine. These chefs learn all they can about a certain cooking style. They prepare meals that have been popular for a long time. Some chefs make small changes to the traditional recipes. This helps them stand out from other chefs who cook in the same style.

A chef can't do all of a restaurant's cooking alone. At some restaurants, the executive or top chef might not do much cooking at all. The other cooks in the kitchen may handle most of the cooking. Most chefs start out as one of these cooks and work their way up to higher positions.

A **sous chef** is the chef under the head chef. He or she supervises the rest of the kitchen staff when the chef is busy with other responsibilities.

21st Century Content

In the past, customers expected their food to be cooked behind closed doors. This is no longer the case! Many restaurants today have open kitchens. This means chefs cook in view of the customers in the restaurants. They can show off how clean their working space is and allow customers to enjoy the wonderful cooking smells. "The dining public wants to see what's going on," said one chef. "Chefs are proud of what we do and like to showcase our habitat."

Many people have different jobs in a restaurant kitchen.

Some restaurants have line, or station, cooks. Each line cook has a station where a certain job is performed. Each station has the tools and ingredients the line cook needs. This helps the cooks quickly prepare many meals at once.

Food preparation workers help the other cooks by doing simple jobs. These include chopping vegetables and measuring ingredients. They might also make sure the kitchen is free of clutter. These jobs help save time for the other cooks.

Chefs handle many different jobs. No matter what chefs do, though, they must know a lot about food and cooking.

Tough but Rewarding

Becoming a chef takes a lot of hard work. Chefs need to learn a variety of special skills. This takes years of practice. Many chefs start their careers by getting on-the-job experience at restaurants. They might start out as dishwashers just to get inside the kitchen. Then they can move into becoming a food preparation worker or line cook, and work their way up from there. Some large restaurants and hotels offer special training programs. In order to move up, cooks need to show that they can work hard. They must prove that they have the skills needed to keep a kitchen running smoothly. It usually takes many years to advance from a beginning cook to a head chef.

Some chefs get their education at culinary arts schools, which teach the skillful preparation of food. There are 578 **accredited**

Many future chefs attend culinary school.

culinary schools in the United States. Students take classes to help them learn basic cooking skills. They learn about knife skills and different ways to cook food. They learn how to use and care for kitchen equipment. Nutrition classes help them learn how to create food that is both healthy and tasty. Classes in menu planning and portion control help prepare them for the duties of a head chef. Other classes teach students how to use ingredients in ways that limit waste. They also learn how to store food so it won't spoil. Most culinary arts programs take between six months and four years. But these schools can be very expensive to attend.

Chefs need to get along with their coworkers in the kitchen.

A two-year program, the most typical length, can cost a total of
$53,000!

Chefs and cooks need strong senses of taste and smell. These
help them figure out which ingredients a recipe needs more or
less of. They also help chefs avoid serving food that tastes bad!
Chefs need to be able to think creatively, too, so they can come
up with recipes that other chefs haven't thought of.

A kitchen can be a stressful place to work. Things move very
quickly. It can be hot, crowded, and loud. Chefs and cooks need
to be able to handle the pressure. They must stay calm even if the

restaurant is very busy or something goes wrong.

Chefs often work long hours—as many as 80 hours a week! They have to be there early in the morning when the deliveries arrive, and they work late into the night for the dinner crowd. But chefs must always stay alert. The kitchen can be a dangerous place for anyone who isn't paying attention. Knives and stoves are important tools, but they can cause cuts and burns.

Life and Career Skills

Eben Copple has been a head chef at a fancy restaurant in Pennsylvania for the past 8 years. He was also a head chef in New York City. He says the three most important skills a chef must have are:

1. *To be able to delegate. "A chef can't do it all. You must make sure to have a good staff working for you in the kitchen."*
2. *To be neat. "Keeping a clean kitchen is super important."*
3. *To be able to stay calm. "Being a chef is stressful, and you have to know how to handle this stress."*

Chefs need to communicate with the waiters who bring the food out to guests.

Chefs need to be able to do many things at once. Sometimes a restaurant has many customers who all want different meals to eat. When this happens, chefs and cooks might need to keep an eye on one dish in the oven while chopping ingredients for a different dish. Being able to pay attention to many things at the same time is crucial. If a chef can't do this, he might make mistakes. Chefs need to be as **efficient** as possible. There is never any time to waste in a busy kitchen.

Kitchen workers need to work well in groups. Food preparation workers and line cooks need to do their jobs quickly so the other cooks aren't delayed. Chefs, sous chefs, and other leaders in the kitchen must pay attention to what everyone is doing. They need to assign jobs to the right people and make sure no steps are forgotten. Everyone must communicate and work together to keep delicious meals flowing out of the kitchen.

21st Century Content

How would you like to eat a meal in total darkness? At Opaque, a restaurant based in California, you don't have a choice. Guests eat in a pitch-black room, staffed by servers who are blind or visually impaired. The experience is supposed to enhance guests' "sense of taste, smell, touch, and hearing by abandoning one that we often take for granted."

Chefs Are Everywhere

The restaurant business is booming! Jobs for chefs are expected to increase by more than 150,000 by 2022. The best chefs will compete for jobs at top restaurants. Only the most talented and creative chefs will find work at these kinds of places.

How much chefs earn depends on where they work and what they do. According to the Bureau of Labor Statistics, most chefs and head cooks start at $23,000 and can make as much as $200,000 a year. Some celebrity chefs make millions of dollars cooking on television shows as well as selling books and recipes. Don't become a chef because you want to become a celebrity, though. Become a chef because you love to prepare and cook good food.

Bobby Flay is a popular modern chef.

Chefs help make dining out an enjoyable experience.

Today's restaurant customers want more specialized choices. They want restaurants that only serve **vegan** or locally grown food. They want **gluten**-free options on the menu. Chefs have to keep up on eating trends and make sure they are serving what their customers want to eat.

Chefs are an important part of our culture. They help shape our tastes and diets. Becoming a successful chef takes a lot of hard work and commitment. But the rewards can be great. Do you have what it takes to make it in this industry?

21st Century Content

According to expert reports based on quality of life and salary, the top five cities to work in as a chef are:
1. Denver, Colorado
2. San Francisco, California
3. Washington, D.C.
4. Bethesda, Maryland
5. Portland, Oregon

Think About It

Ask your mom or dad if you can help them cook something in the kitchen. Do they follow a recipe, or do they make it up as they go along? Was this meal easier or harder to cook than you imagined? Write a paragraph about the experience, how the food turned out, and how you could improve it next time.

Go to the website www.pbs.org/food/shows. Browse through all the cooking shows that are available to watch. Try watching one of them. What tips did you learn?

Do you think it is important for chefs to always try to cook meals that are as healthy as possible? Why or why not?

For More Information

BOOKS

Liebman, Dan. *I Want to Be a Chef.* Richmond Hill, ON: Firefly Books, 2012.

Murdoch Books. *I Want to Be a Chef: Baking.* Melbourne, Australia: Murdoch Books, 2012.

Witherspoon, Jack. *Twist It Up: More Than 60 Delicious Recipes from an Inspiring Young Chef.* San Francisco: Chronicle Books, 2011.

WEB SITES

American Culinary Federation
www.acfchefs.org
Visit this Web site to learn more about apprenticeships and culinary education.

Chefs for Kids
www.chefsforkids.org
Learn more about this organization that teaches kids healthy eating habits.

KidsHealth—Recipes and Cooking
www.kidshealth.org/kid/recipes/index.html
Try your hand at being a chef with these recipes. Be sure to have an adult help.

GLOSSARY

accredited (ah-KRED-ih-tid) given official approval for teaching

complement (KOM-pluh-muhnt) to go well with

cuisine (kwi-ZEEN) a style or way of cooking or presenting food

efficient (uh-FISH-uhnt) able to work well without wasting energy or time

farm-to-table (FAHRM-too-TAY-buhl) a style of restaurant where the ingredients are bought from local farms instead of imported from far away

gluten (GLOOT-en) a substance in wheat that makes the dough more elastic; it can make people sick if they are allergic to it

health codes (HELTH KOHDZ) rules set up by a local government for how a kitchen must be kept clean and organized in order to prevent sickness

marinades (MAIR-uh-naydz) flavorful liquids in which foods are soaked before cooking

menu (MEN-yoo) a list of foods served at a restaurant

regional (REE-juh-nuhl) having to do with a certain area

serrated (SER-ay-tid) having notches or teeth like a saw

sous chef (SOO SHEF) the second in command to a head chef in a kitchen

sous vide (SOO VEED) the technique of cooking ingredients in a vacuum-sealed bag

textures (TEKS-churz) the feel, appearance, or consistency of a surface or a substance

vegan (VEE-guhn) containing no animal products

vegetarian (vej-ih-TAIR-ee-uhn) consisting of only plants and plant products and sometimes eggs or dairy products

INDEX